IN OLD PHOTOG BRITAIN

CHANGING ASHFORD

STEVE R. SALTER

Steve Salter 2003

SUTTON PUBLISHING

Sutton Publishing Limited
Phoenix Mill · Thrupp · Stroud
Gloucestershire · GL5 2BU

First published 2003

Title page: Aerial view, 1981. An interesting view of the town centre before traffic was totally banned. St Mary's Church and churchyard dominate the foreground, the Tufton Centre can be seen top left and the Upper and Lower High Streets on the right. (*Weavers/Countrywide*)

British Library Cataloguing in Publication Data
A catalogue record for this book is available from the British Library.

ISBN 0-7509-3714-9

Typeset in 10.5/13.5 Photina.
Typesetting and origination by
Sutton Publishing Limited.
Printed and bound in England by
J.H. Haynes & Co. Ltd, Sparkford.

Dedicated to Mum, Dad, Nan and Fred

Station Road, 6 November 1974. Now part of the Ringway, Station Road is quite narrow compared with today's road. Kent House can be seen at the junction of Tannery Lane, while the houses in the centre were later demolished to make way for the Royal Mail sorting office, seen here at the bottom next to the former South Kent College site. Towards the top right behind the houses the Stour Centre is under construction. The pitched roofed timber building opposite the houses in the centre was once Ashford Library. (*Weavers/Countrywide*)

CONTENTS

/ellesley Road, 1973. hese properties were emolished in 1974 to eate Park Street ervice road. Emetco, at o. 22, is still trading sewhere in the town. he company's speciality domestic and dustrial electrical oducts. *ambert Weston)*

Bank Street, July 1952. Still recognisable today are the offices of Hallett & Co., solicitors, which have dominated upper Bank Street for many years, although the premises look much smarter today. Curry's Cycle Co. moved from here several years later, to create additional office space for the solicitors. (*Weavers/Countrywide*)

INTRODUCTION

In the past half-century Ashford has undergone a substantial and controversial change of image. Many newcomers to the town have no idea of just how much change there has been since the 1950s. It would be fair to say it would take a true Ashfordian to chart how these changes affected everyday lives. It was quite a traumatic experience living there at the beginning of the major alterations to this once quaint and sleepy Kentish market town. Long forgotten are those streets and properties which were once local landmarks. For example, there were many more public houses within the town centre not so long ago. Quite a proportion of these disappeared all at once, in the early '70s. Familiar traders and businesses such as Lewis & Hyland, W.H. Gibbs, Knowles and Internationals, to name but a few, have vanished in the name of progress. Once close-knit streets and communities moved out for the bulldozers and caused at the time something of a housing crisis, because of the lack of residential property. These people and their families knew that their everyday lives in Ashford would never be the same again.

The population of the town centre also changed considerably in the 1960s, with many families from London moving into the town from their already fast-expanding city. This development was commonly known as the 'London overspill'. Next year is the thirtieth anniversary of Ashford's borough status; 1974 was also a key year in the redevelopment of the town. Large construction projects included a new local office for a mining finance company, Charter Consolidated Ltd, which already occupied an overcrowded Kent House in Station Road; the Tufton Centre, which was constructed on a largely derelict area covering Hempsted Street and Tufton Street; and the controversial Ringway, which after twenty-eight years is still the subject of much argument and complaint, and to date has eighteen sets of traffic lights. It was criticised for its 'Brands Hatch'-style design, and the fact that it isolated the centre of town. These developments all played their part in the upheaval of the town centre at this time.

Upper High Street, 16 April 1970. A busy spring scene showing the street before the construction of th Ringway. Buses still had to negotiate their way past the Castle Inn in the centre. Lewis & Hyland's menswea department can be seen to the left of the double-decker bus. This store, and all its adjoining propertie stretching along New Rents, was later demolished to make room for the Tufton Centre, later rename County Square. The International Stores to the right was demolished in 1986 to create the entrance to Par Mall shopping centre.

This collection of many unseen and unpublished illustrations, which has been collected and built up over the last seventeen years, portrays the town from the 1950s to the present day. These photographs create an interesting and sometimes sentimental, nostalgic even, look at Ashford in a largely forgotten period. It is particularly fortunate that many of these photographs have been dated on the reverse, so while browsing through this book you will be able to pinpoint exactly where you were in Ashford at that time.

Steve R. Salter
Ashford
October 2003

1

Ashford's Forgotten Familiarities

Upper High Street, looking towards Kings Parade and Middle Row, 1970. The Commercial Union building on the right (with the protruding flagpole) once housed Photocraft Studios and the *Kentish Express* office. Brighter Homes, Bateman's Opticians and Hepworth's tailors can be seen to the left of the Commercial Union building. Also on the right are Lewis & Hyland, who had a later department store, now Peacocks, in the Tufton Centre. (*Roy Entwistle*)

Upper High Street, 1970. This alleyway ran alongside 91–93 High Street, Lewis & Hyland's shop, right down to Godinton Road. The window on the left is to the rear of the head post office in Tufton Street, and the Bank Street Methodist Church can be seen in the distance.

Below: Upper High Street, 1969. Taken from the junction of Bank Street and the High Street, this view shows no. 83, Hepworth's men's tailors on the left and James & Kither, H. Horton and Son Shoes and International Stores on the right. Notice the traffic lights outside Hepworth's.

Upper High Street, 1972. This photograph was probably taken on a Sunday: note the lack of traffic and pedestrians. Record Corner was for many years renowned both for its records and audio equipment. The shop continued trading on this site until the late 1970s, when Our Price records took over the site. Next door, Knowles the furnishers also traded on this site for many years. The building was later redeveloped and for a considerable time the National and Provincial Building Society occupied the building.

Upper High Street from approximately the same position as the scene above, 1973. The Castle Inn is on the left, together with a pedestrianised Upper High Street. New Rents in the foreground has since been pedestrianised.

Upper High Street/Castle Street, 1972. Apart from the building nearest the camera, nos 103 (Gibbs Carpets), 105 (Foster Brothers, menswear) and 107 (F. Gutteridge, chemist), all later made way for Marks & Spencer and phase two of the Tufton Shopping Centre.

Below: The Castle Hotel, 1 Castle Street, 1974. Many Ashfordians will remember the Castle Hotel, or the Castle Inn as it was later known, in its more recent existence as a bikers' pub; but sadly it closed in 1996. Subsequently Halifax plc bought the property and opened their bank in 1997 after extensive rebuilding and refurbishment. They also retained much of the traditional pub-style frontage.

The junction of Upper High Street junction and New Rents, 1974. Immediately to the left at no. 109 is Charles Warner, the butcher (previously Brickies). Next door at nos. 111–13 is Frank Palmer's men's outfitter advertising its closing down sale. This shop stood at the junction of New Rents and Hempsted Street. On the opposite corner at 1–3 New Rents Nicholas Kingsman the baker was next door to nos 5–15, Lewis & Hyland's store, which once dominated New Rents. Not one building in this photograph is left standing today.

Below: Upper High Street, December 1975. Commercial Union House is on the left and K Shoes and Marcus Stores on the right. Adjacent to the bus shelter is the newly opened Tufton Centre. Commercial Union House became Roselodge Kitchens in the 1980s, but at the time of this photograph was home to Bishop's insurance brokers, Vine's estate agents and Mace Windsor, solicitors. It is currently occupied by the Body Shop and Starbuck's Coffee.

Upper High Street, 1976. John Farmer shoes and Richard Shops proudly front the Tufton Centre in this post pedestrianised photograph. It is difficult to imagine that just a year earlier this street was a busy traffic area The International Stores is on the right at nos 92–94, promoting double Green Shield Stamps in the 1970s Many businesses offered these stamps as an incentive for shopping, or sometimes petrol. The bulldozed Lewi & Hyland's site stands ready for phase two of the Tufton Centre, which was yet to get under way.

Upper High Street, 1977. This is a familiar view to many. Within a year the council had introduced plantin and seating to the newly pedestrianised area. With this section of the High Street no longer needed as main thoroughfare for traffic, it made a pleasant alternative, allowing shoppers to roam freely.

Jo. 102 Upper High Street, 1980. 'reviously the Co-op chemist and the 'arpet Centre, Matthew's butchers uffered a near disaster when the shop's luminated sign caught light, owing to n electrical fault. After changing wnership to Dewhurst in the late 80s, no. 102 has been a sports shop, nd more recently became a Zoom the oom outlet.

Below: Upper High Street, 1983. Here is typical scene from the early 1980s. 'hase two of the Tufton Centre is omplete, clearly showing Marks & pencer (centre) and its adjoining remises in New Rents. An acquired oard has been fixed to nos 92–94. After a few years International Stores vas demolished to make way for the 'ark Mall shopping centre.

A deserted Upper High Street on a rainy day in 1987, looking towards Kings Parade and Middle Row. Woolworth's, Geerings, Olivers and Burton's menswear can be seen on the left. Boots Cookshop has been demolished ready for a new W.H. Smith. Over a year later the street paving was totally redesigned and new seating was installed. (*R.G. Salter*)

Upper High Street, 1989. The transformed paving and seating further enhanced the High Street, which was altered again in the late 1990s.

New Street, 1969. A pre-Ringway look at this street from the Prince Albert public house looking towards the town centre. R. Passmore & Sons, the builders' merchants, can be seen on the left, at no. 74, which later became David Easton's radio and TV shop. Further down on the left is the British Volunteer public house. Next door Violet Perkins had a grocer's shop for many years, but this sadly closed after the opening of Safeway's opposite in 1986. On the right is 'Skip' Hudson's cycle shop and E.C. Wellman's rag and metal yard.

New Street, 1974. For many years Sonny Hanson ran a fish and chip shop and restaurant on the corner of New Street and Gilbert Road. Sonny was a well-known figure in the town. Later his nephew Bill Saltmarsh ran the restaurant until 1985. It is now a quality furniture and antique store by the name of Bakudi. Sonny lived in two houses at Penlee Point, Canterbury Road, Kennington, one of which is now the St Valery nursing home; the other, Creg-ny-baa (named after part of the Isle of Man TT racing circuit), was demolished in 1999 after standing unoccupied for ten years. The land made way for an access road to the new Little Burton Farm estate.

New Street, Goddard's butchers, 1950s. Goddard's was renowned for decades as a quality butcher. The shop was an unusual shape, allowing them to put on displays of meat and poultry products. Shown here are Tony Ansell (standing left) and Mr Goddard (standing centre); the gentleman on the right and the van driver are sadly unidentified. The van's registration is YKL 108.

New Street, 1974. Here is another view of Goddard's, showing the familiar curved shop frontage. Tony Ansell continued to run the business until his death a few years ago. In 2000 the Goddard's name disappeared, and Quality Meats traded here for just under a year.

New Street/Castle Street, 1974. Further down from Goddard's stood Merry's newsagents, R. Dean turf accountant (previously in Park Street), Knowles, Oxfam and the Castle Inn, all of which were in Castle Street.

New Street, 1969. The Tank Milk Bar will be fondly remembered by Ashfordians of this era. Mr E. Collins ran the milk bar for many years. Since then the premises have been taken over by a variety of businesses, including Indian and Bangladeshi restaurants. Daniel's estate agents and auctioneers were at 7 New Street; next door was Goulden's wools and fancy goods and also Jack Scott's secondhand bargain shop. On the opposite corner to Hanson's was A. Sellers, the well-known local butchers.

New Street, 1974. Only five years later and Daniel's estate agents have disappeared and Goulden's have closed, making way for Jack Scott's bargain shop, which also took over no. 9.

New Rents/Forge Lane, 1974. This view was taken from the top of New Rents and Gravel Walk car park. Lewis & Hyland's can be seen below the church tower at 5–15 New Rents. H.J. Davis, the pork butcher, stands next door at 21 New Rents, while no. 23 is occupied by F.G. Bradley, the yeast merchant and bakers' sundriesman.

New Street, 1983. Before the road alterations in the 1970s Caffyn's occupied part of the land, which became Gravel Walk car park. Many drivers will remember filling up with fuel opposite their main showroom. Three years after this photograph was taken Safeway's built a brand new supermarket on the site, which continued trading until its closure in 1997. The original supermarket building was split and now houses Fitness First gym and a Lidl supermarket.

New Street, 1987. A deserted Caffyn's Garage awaits its fate. Caffyn's had occupied the premises since 1967; they had previously been owned by the well-known business C. Hayward & Son, who had been on the site for many decades. Caffyn's had moved to Henwood when this photograph was taken, to allow demolition to take place. This site was initially sought by Lidl, but remained a temporary car park for ten years after which three large shop units were built.

Opposite: New Street, 1974. A rare view, looking towards Maidstone Road before the roundabout was constructed. The Prince Albert and Prince of Orange public houses are on the left. Further up on the left stood Leaver's the tobacconist and confectioner. The road junction on the right is Magazine Road, where there once stood a water tower and a brickworks. Next to the road junction stood St Teresa's Roman Catholic Church, designed by Edward Pugin, which was demolished in the 1980s and replaced with a building of modern design. The houses on the right were demolished shortly after this photograph was taken, for the new roundabout. (*Kentish Express*)

New Street/Magazine Road, 1974. These houses stood opposite the Magazine Road junction before the construction of the roundabout. In the middle of the row stood Leaver's the tobacconist and confectioner, run by Mr C.J. Leaver, who also had shops in Middle Row and Bank Street. Upon his death his son David continued running the Middle Row shop with his wife Anne, until recently, when the shop was purchased by new owners, continuing trade with Anne's friendly service. (*Richard Filmer*)

New Street, 1975. Demolition contractors have already stripped the roofs of the properties including Leaver's, all destined to be bulldozed shortly after this photograph was taken. (*Kentish Express*)

New Street, 1975. Philip Clark was a well-known flooring specialist throughout the 1970s and '80s, having shops in Bank Street, New Rents and, as seen in this view, New Street, in the Old Vineyard drive-in off-licence at nos 14–16. Also in this area Geerings had their office furniture warehouse. Sadly Philip Clark died a few years ago; I believe his son was keen to continue his father's trade.

Barrow Hill, 1972. In this peaceful setting, just behind the Prince of Orange in New Street, are Engineers Place and Gravel Walk (to the left) and also Barrow Hill Cottages. The building on the right was once known as a school for naughty girls. Apart from the change of road surface and the demolition of Engineers Place, this area looks much the same today.

New Rents looking west towards Forge Lane from its junction with Hempsted Street, 1972. Difficult for many to remember and almost totally unrecognisable today, Lewis & Hyland's department store dominated much of the left-hand side of New Rents. Above Lewis & Hyland's the sign clearly shows Hartley's Hair Fashions. Just before the gap at the top left is H.J. Davis, pork butcher, and opposite is Kennard's music shop, now the Music Shop. Other traders in New Rents at this time were Gerald Brown, greengrocer, Dekor Discount, the Fabric Shop and the Central Pie Shop. The building on the immediate left is Nicholas Kingsman, the baker, run by Mr and Mrs Weekes. Almost everything on the left-hand side was later demolished for the Tufton Centre.

Hempsted Street, 1972. This forgotten view is looking towards the side of the Castle Inn and the junction with New Rents. The building on the right in the distance was Frank Palmer's men's outfitters. Dann's secondhand shop can be seen on the immediate right at 3 Hempsted Street. Nos 5, 7, 9 and 11, together with most of the other buildings in Hempsted Street, were derelict at this time. Just behind the camera was the site of the Friends' Meeting House.

New Rents, 1973. Much of the property on the left looks familiar today but every building on the right was to disappear days after this photograph was taken. Gerald Brown's greengrocer's, Dekor Discount, H.J. Davis, pork butcher, and Lewis & Hyland's can be clearly seen. In the distance, Frank Palmer's shop at 111–13 High Street has already been demolished.

Middle Row, 1968. This interesting scene shows some of the town's lost trades. Dixon's ironmongers (now part of the Man of Kent public house) was a well-known trader within the town for over seventy-five years. It was apparently one of the first businesses in Ashford to have a telephone. In older photographs the shop's wares – including tools, domestic hardware, garden and dairy requisites, saucepans and tin baths – were hung outside the door. To the left Bodsham's farm shop trades from the former Waghorne butcher's shop, and Rumbelows TV rentals became Multi Broadcast in the early 1980s.

Middle Row, 1968. Further to the left J. Sainsbury's second supermarket is shown under construction. Previously the Saracen's Head Hotel had stood on the site but it was demolished in 1966. The local construction firm C.I. Epps was the contractor for the new building, which replaced Sainsbury's store at 18 High Street.

Middle Row, 1981. One of the smallest streets in the town looks the worse for wear. The busy street had to put up with heavy drays delivering ale to the Man of Kent over the years. Since pedestrianisation the street looks much the same apart from the difference in trade. The greengrocer's on the left is now the New Ashford Bookshop, Town and Country Kitchens is now Adecco Recruitment Agency, the estate agents is now the Tanning Shop, and the building with the overhanging gable is now a popular restaurant and take-away, The Chilli Bite, mainly specialising in South African cuisine. This building is one of the oldest in the town.

The junction of Lower High Street with North Street, 1983. Lower High Street had been partly pedestrianised at the time of this picture, taken from outside Boots the Chemist. The building on the corner of North Street advertising a sale is John Collier's men's tailor, whose slogan for many years was 'The Window to Watch'. Opposite is Ward and Partners estate agents, with its fancy decorative plasterwork known as pargetting; this building has a cellar which many years ago served as the old town gaol, also known as 'the cage'. Nature's Way to the right was later taken over by Holland & Barrett health foods.

Lower High Street, 1976. The Lower High Street once joined with East Hill to act as the main road from Ashford to Folkestone. It is said to be one of the widest high streets in the country and during the 1940s cars were allowed to park centrally, and traffic still had enough space to flow freely on either side. By the time this photograph was taken it had been made one-way in the direction of East Hill, with buses serving the left-hand side and domestic traffic the right. (*Kentish Express*)

MIDLAND BANK
SCOTT
KENDON

ODEON

the window to watch
BOYDS
OF BOND STREET
DEWHURST
CHOCOLATE BOX
CIGARS

Lower High Street, 1976. Marshalls Fashions at 16 High Street was a familiar name for ladieswear in the 1970s, as were Ashley Russell, James & Kither and Lewis & Hyland. This picture clearly shows the dismay on the lady's face at the thought of Marshall's closing down; she is believed to have been a regular customer. (*Kentish Express*)

Lower High Street, 1983. The pedestrian area in Lower High Street was fully pedestrianised in the late 1990s, allowing outdoor café seating and the installation of a fountain.

Opposite above: Lower High Street, 1969. This is an earlier view showing the High Street in the spring. The shops on the bottom right, including Olby's and Lee and Son, are present at this time, to be replaced a few years later by Pearl Assurance House. On the left Headley Brothers, the grocers, Ingall and Son, chemists, Photocraft and the individual Co-operative Stores still remain. The Odeon, which opened in 1936, later changed to a Rank bingo hall. Next door the estate agents Scott Kendon and Ronald Pearce occupied St John's Chambers. The company later became just Scott and Kendon and was taken over by Halifax in 1988.

Opposite below: Lower High Street, 1976. Nos 48–50 and 52 High Street are seen here together with their interesting displays. Boyds of Bond Street was a TV and radio specialist, here advertising 'Home Entertainment Discount Bargains'. Dewhurst, the butchers, a name that disappeared from the town in the late 1980s, are to the right. The only business in this picture still trading is the Chocolate Box.

Lower High Street, 1983. Here is another view showing the taxi rank in the Lower High Street. Scott & Kendon estate agents, Pickford's Travel, Gizzi Restaurant and Café are familiar names of the 1980s.

Lower High Street, 1987. The High Street in the late 1980s, looking towards the Upper High Street. The stone in the flowerbed was unveiled in 1985 by Herr Ferdinand Lethert, the mayor of Ashford's twin town, Bad Munsterifiel. (*R.G. Salter*)

Lower High Street, 1974. The County Hotel was for many years a popular hotel and banqueting venue. It once boasted a large restaurant and a professionally sprung dance floor, at one time said to be the best in the area. In 1997 J.D. Wetherspoon refurbished the former hotel and reopened it in February 1998 as a music-free public house. (*Kentish Express*)

Lower High Street, February 1998. The newly refurbished County Hotel reopens for business, although the original hotel rooms have never since been used. The County now boasts a pleasant patio area with outdoor heaters and extensive internal seating. Despite Wetherspoon's policy of no music, they have proved that the art of conversation in their countrywide establishments makes for a refreshing change.

Kings Parade, December 1972. A rare view looking towards the Lower High Street and Middle Row, showing the town's first Christmas lights in the days before pedestrianisation. Timothy Whites can be seen on the left next to the George Hotel. The shops illustrated on the right are Stuarts ladies' fashions, Milletts, Knevetts Bakery and the South Eastern Electricity Board shop (Seeboard).

Lower High Street, December 1972. Another view of the Christmas lights, looking towards the Odeon and Pearl Assurance House. These days the former Odeon houses a Mecca bingo hall. Pearl Assurance later changed its name when the company was bought by Australian insurers AMP and moved to another location. The building is now known as Northdown House.

Lower High Street, December 1972. This view has been taken from the High Street's junction with Station Road. Barclays Bank is on the left and Pricerite, the National Westminster Bank and Marshalls Fashions are on the right.

ank Street, December 1972. The hotographer is looking from the top f Bank Street towards Tufton Street. loyds Bank and Geering & Colyer re on the left, while Hepworth's, ateman's Opticians and Iutchinson's radio shop are on the ight.

ower High Street, December 1976. . later view showing the part-edestrianised street and the bright vindow displays. Many will emember the curved advertising oards which were situated in arious locations around the town uring the 1970s and early '80s. hese disappeared before the redesign f the pedestrianised areas in the igh Street.

ank Street, December 1985. n attractive view of another hristmas display, showing a traffic-ned Bank Street before the troduction of new bus stops and e removal of the pelican crossing utside the Methodist Church. *.G. Salter)*

Bank Street, July 1953. The attractive offices of Hallett & Co., solicitors, are seen here with their floral window boxes. At one time the Royal Insurance Company occupied the former Curry Cycle Co. premises, and later the Royal Insurance Co. moved to the corner of Bank Street and Tufton Street – illustrated here approximately where the motorbike can be seen. At this time the street had two-way traffic and East Kent buses stopped outside Hallett & Co. Next door G. Herbert and Co., jewellers, pawnbrokers and outfitters, stood where Richard's Records now have their successful shop. (*Weavers/Countrywide*)

Bank Street, July 1953. Another look at the offices of Hallett and Co., showing typical 1950s dress and hairstyles. To the far left the entrance to Kingsford, Flower and Pain, solicitors, can be seen, and to the right G. Herbert, the jewellers, boast that they are 'Dealers in Diamonds and Precious Stones'. The street has since been pedestrianised. (*Weavers/Countrywide*)

Bank Street, 1988. The traffic had been made one-way, in the direction of the High Street, by the early 1960s, and here bus stops line the left-hand side of Bank Street. Gizzi's can be seen to the left, a familiar name in the town for over thirty years. Antonio Gizzi and his wife Vilma also ran a restaurant in the Lower High Street, extremely popular with both business people and shoppers at lunchtimes. In the late 1980s their Bank Street café closed but the Gizzis continued to run their successful High Street restaurant and café. Cobbs estate agents later became Just Jeans and Ashford People a mobile phone outlet.

'ufton Street, 1972. The Elwick
'lub was once situated next to the
nain post office in Tufton Street. At
ne time it was a men-only venue,
ut in 1975 it was ruled that
vomen should be allowed into the
lub. Opposite were the Almshouses,
vhich, together with the club, were
emolished in 1973 to make way for
he Tufton Centre. After demolition
he club moved to new premises in
'hurch Road near the library, and
ew Almshouses were built in
'icarage Lane opposite the Bowling
ireen.

he junction of Hempsted Street with Tufton Street, 1972. The Coach & Horses public house stood on the
orner of Hempsted Street and was for many years a familiar haunt for locals. In the background is the
elephone Exchange, built in 1963. Shortly after this photograph was taken Hempsted Street was bulldozed
preparation for the Tufton Centre.

DANNS
SALE

Hempsted Street, 1973. A rare and almost forgotten view of Hempsted Street shortly before it was bulldozed. Looking towards New Rents, this view shows businesses including Dann's secondhand shop, the Shoe Box and, on the corner with New Rents, Nicholas Kingsman the bakers, who later acquired premises within the Tufton Shopping Centre. Incidentally, the dark rendered building behind the two gentlemen was at this time the Castle Hotel. None of the traders featured in this photograph is still in business today.

Stone Street, 1971. The Park Hotel on the corner of Stone Street and Wolseley Road was one of Ashford's many inns lost in the redevelopment plans of the 1970s. The Park Mall shopping centre now stands on this site. (*Kentish Express*)

Park Street, 1976. Here is a familiar view from the mid-1970s, although much of this area today has been pedestrianised. The Lord Roberts public house once stood between these two buildings. With the redevelopment of the area for Charter House, a service road was required for access, so Park Street was subsequently widened and many buildings had to be demolished. On the left is W.H. Gibbs' house furnishers and removal contractors. The building is now a Pizza Express restaurant. Denne, the seed merchant on the right, closed in the 1980s and sadly suffered a fire in 1997. After standing derelict for six and a half years the building is now under reconstruction.

New Street, 1974. Nos 21–23 New Street were once the offices of F. Knock & Co., builders and undertakers. It was also many years ago the offices for the *Kentish Express*. Since 1983 Peter S. Roberts, insurance brokers, have occupied the building.

St George's Square, 1983. The First World War tank, given to the town on 1 August 1919, can be seen here with the New China City Restaurant and the Old Prince of Wales public house. In 1988 a protective cover was constructed for the old tank, which for many years housed an electricity sub-station.

Gasworks Lane looking towards Godinton Road, 1972. Until recent years Gasworks Lane connected with Victoria Park and was used as a thoroughfare for Ashford cattle market. The Elephant & Castle public house can be seen on the corner of Apsley Street and Godinton Road; in recent years it was converted into Oranges Café Bar, a thriving venue for live music. Upon construction of the Channel Tunnel rail link Gasworks Lane was realigned and the cattle market moved to the Orbital Park at Sevington.

North Street, 1983. At the time of this photograph the premises of W.H. Gibbs the house furnishers and removal contractors in North Street were vacant. The business next door, Ashford Sports, later moved into the old W.H. Gibbs showroom, and their former premises became the Coliseum a few years later. The Olde Cottage Restaurant has since changed hands many times, and is now the Little Raj Indian restaurant.

Park Street, 1983. Folkestone Glassworks stood opposite the tank in St George's Square on the junction with Park Street and Park Road. Most of the surrounding buildings and properties were demolished in 1985 to make way for the Park Mall shopping centre, leaving this building standing alone for several years.

Church Road, 1975. The Congregational Church once stood on the corner of Church Road and Tufton Street. It closed in August 1971 and is seen here being dismantled. The site of the former church later housed a new Magistrates Court. (*Kentish Express*)

Norwood Street, 1976. The construction of the new Magistrates Court is seen here in its early stages. The buildings in the foreground beyond the brick wall are the workshops for the old T/4 Kent Police traffic area, at Ashford police station.

Tannery Lane, looking east, before the construction of the Stour Centre, March 1972. Kent House can just be seen on the immediate left, and further down is Orchard House, which was occupied respectively by the Ministry of Fishery and Agriculture, Department of Social Security, the County Courts and the Ordnance Survey. The entrance to Kent Wool Growers is indicated on the right beyond the high wall.

Tannery Lane, 27 September 1972. Seven months after the above photograph was taken the new access for the proposed Stour Centre was beginning to take shape. The Stour Centre opened in 1975 and the Civic Centre was later built next door, opening in December 1983.

Tannery Lane, 1973. Construction of the Stour Centre was hampered by bad weather in 1973. Its situation next to the River Stour made it more or less a flood plain, as can be clearly seen in this photograph. The rear of the Rank, Hovis, McDougall factory can be seen in the background.

Tannery Lane, 1975. The Stour Centre was opened by Mayor Cllr Peter G. Boulden on 15 February 1975. One of the town's previous leisure facilities was a large open-air swimming pool in Beaver Road, now Beaver Commercials. Talks are currently under way regarding the refurbishment of the centre, including the provision of an updated larger pool.

East Hill, 16 February 1974. The flour mills in East Hill have been for many years a popular landmark. The main six-storey tower was built in 1901 and the mill house and provender mill illustrated are much older. Henry Sturges Pledge, who owned the mill, also owned Victoria Mills alongside the South Eastern Railway line. He started business in the old mill behind the Golden Ball public house in Kennington. East Hill Mill had closed by 1972, and was up for sale with local agents Burrows & Co. This was probably one of the last pictures to be taken of the older mill. (*Leonard Harman estate*)

Below: East Hill Mill, 16 May 1974. The local police called in Scotland Yard detectives to determine the cause of the fire. At the time it was rumoured by the local press that youths were seen venturing inside the mill at about 6 p.m. on the evening of 16 May. It was also common knowledge that the empty mill was a haven for vandals. The mill remained a burned-out shell for eight years afterwards. (*Dennis Shadwell*)

East Hill, 16 May 1974. Another view of the suspicious blaze at East Hill Mill. Local residents crowded the bottom of East Hill to watch the familiar landmark disappear, and palls of smoke could be seen as far away as Wye. Thanks to the efforts of the fire brigade, the six-storey tower and the barrel-vaulted warehouse were saved. Sadly, the remains of the older mill and the mill house had to be demolished. At the time East Hill was part of the main Ashford to Folkestone Road. (*Dennis Shadwell*)

East Hill Mill, 1981. The gutted shell of the flour mills was purchased in 1981, and rebuilt to create Ashford's first nightclub, Dusty's. The club was once owned by businessman Lakshman Pigera who ran it only for a short while before being highlighted by the local press after disappearing, owing thousands of pounds. The complex also included a banqueting suite, together with the Jolly Miller public house and restaurant. In 1990 Kingfisher Leisure refurbished the club and renamed the venue Cale's and Flatfoot Sam's. They both closed in 2001, and Luminar Leisure, the new owners, spent £4 million to create superclub Liquid and Life; and also creating a trouble-free venue. (*Kentish Express*)

The junction of Magazine Road with Canterbury Road, 1981. Totally unrecognisable today, this is the junction prior to the installation of traffic lights, which was carried out as a safety measure owing to the number of accidents at this spot. To the left the road goes towards Kennington, and right towards North Street and the town centre.

Magazine Road, 1981. An old Ford Cortina heads towards the junction with Canterbury Road. In the days before the installation of traffic lights, the Canterbury Road end of Magazine Road seemed as if it should have been in the countryside, as it was very narrow and overgrown. The junction was also extensively widened, a necessity given today's increased volume of traffic.

2

Development is the Key Word

Godinton Road/Hempsted Street, 1972. This view is taken from the derelict land in Hempsted Street, looking towards the rear of Bank Street. The land is being cleared for the Tufton Centre, which opened in 1975. To the far left the Elwick Club and the post office can be seen in Tufton Street. The buildings under demolition near the post office are the old almshouses. Ashford Motors can be seen in the centre, in Middle Street, while the rear of Bank Street Methodist Church and the Centrepiece youth club can be seen on the right. (*Kentish Express*)

Godinton Road, 1972. Not instantly recognisable today, this view is taken from Hempsted Street looking towards Hempsted Terrace in Godinton Road. In the foreground are the remains of the cellars that belonged to the properties already demolished in Hempsted Street. Some of the businesses illustrated are Newman's Secondhand Department, the Market Tobacco Stores, Norman Brett's greengrocer's and Gordon's newsagent's. Today this site is a car park, but plans are under way to build an extension to County Square (formerly the Tufton Centre). (*Kentish Express*)

Godinton Road at its junction with Hempsted Street, 1972: another view looking to the rear of the Bank Street Methodist Church. Beyond Ashford Motors is the post office and the Elwick Club. The building with the four sash windows was Flynn's the cleaners, which later became a Wimpy bar. (*Kentish Express*)

The junction of Hempsted Street and Middle Street, 1972. This closer view of Hempsted Street shows the substantial demolition in progress. The Wellington Hotel is on the left (the tall white building) at the junction with Tufton Street. The Elwick Club can be seen on the right; the main building was built in 1922 and extended in 1930. The almshouses can be seen opposite the Elwick Club, and were later replaced by new ones in Vicarage Lane. (*Kentish Express*)

Tufton Street, 1973. The foundations for the new shopping centre are in place. Bank Street Methodist Church can be seen in the background. (*Kentish Express*)

Hempsted Street, 1973: an interesting view taken from the roof of the telephone exchange in Regent's Place. Charter House can be seen in the background screened by scaffolding and cranes. The rear of 5–15 New Rents (Lewis & Hyland) can be seen on the left, as can the Castle Inn and the Upper High Street. The roofless menswear department of Lewis & Hyland and Lloyds Bank are on the right. Ashtower Warehouse Co. is bottom left. (*Richard Carley*)

Upper High Street, August 1974. The former premises of butcher Charles Warner at 109 High Street are seen here being demolished. The building of the Tufton Centre is already in progress: the contractors were Fairweather of London.

Upper High Street, August 1974. Here is another view looking towards the front of 109 High Street, much of which was timber. The concrete shuttering for the entrance to the Tufton Centre is on the right.

Aerial view, 1973. This shot gives a better perspective of the vast construction projects undertaken at this time. In the centre is the foundation stage of the Tufton Centre; centre left is Tufton Street, where the Elwick Club is being demolished. The Coach & Horses public house stands alone at the bottom of the picture near the telephone exchange. The Upper High Street, New Rents and New Street are to the left. In the top left of the photograph the Stour Centre is under construction. (*Weavers/Countrywide*)

RECORD CORNER
KNOWLES
FAIRWEATHER

Aerial view, 1975. The new shopping centre is nearing completion. Bank Street runs from top to bottom at the right of the picture; Godinton Road runs parallel with the Ringway at the bottom; and the Upper High Street runs along the top, connecting with New Rents, top left. The Invicta public house is situated at the bottom behind the shopping centre; it has since been demolished, together with the row of houses, shops and the Wig and Gavel public house at the bottom in Godinton Road. (*Weavers/Countrywide*)

Regents Place, 1973. This superb view gives a memorable view of the construction of the Tufton Centre. Again taken from the roof of the telephone exchange, it shows the main foundations taking shape on the site of a once-residential area. Middle Street can be seen top left. Godinton Road runs along the right-hand side of the picture, and the houses in the foreground are in Apsley Street. (*Richard Carley*)

New Rents looking towards Forge Lane, December 1975. Nicholas Kingsman at 1–3 New Rents, the former bakery, and Lewis & Hyland at 5–15 New Rents have been demolished by the time of this picture. Roger Britton Carpets at one time used the remaining section of the Lewis & Hyland building.

Upper High Street, December 1975. This is the High Street entrance to the new Tufton Centre, showing two of the original stores. John Farmer later became Clarks Shoes and Richard Shops later changed their name to Richard's. In 1993, when Richard's closed, Clinton Cards moved from their store in the Park Mall shopping centre. The absence of Marks & Spencer is apparent, their new store not yet built.

Centre Square, the Tufton Centre, December 1975. This pleasant open courtyard is at the heart of the new Tufton Centre. Lewis & Hyland's replacement ladieswear department is seen in the centre, while two new stores have come to Ashford, Tesco Home 'n' Wear, over two floors, and H. Samuel, jewellers, to the right.

South Mall, the Tufton Centre, December 1975. Another of the main supermarket chains of the 1970s, Presto, will be remembered not only for its supermarket but also its Carlton Restaurant on the upper floor, which was something of a treat in 1975.

Godinton Road, 1975. During the redevelopment of the 1970s many of the familiar public houses were lost – including the Wellington, the Coach and Horses, the Somerset Arms and the Lord Roberts – so upon construction of the Tufton Centre it was decided to create the Zodiac public house, to the south end of the shopping centre. The Zodiac closed in 1988 just before the shopping centre was refurbished.

outh Square, the Tufton
entre, 1975. The open-air
esign of the Tufton Centre
reated a pleasant
hopping atmosphere. Two
f the shops in the South
quare, Dalgety frozen
oods and Mothercare, are
hown here.

entre Square, the Tufton
entre, 1975. Apart from
he shops and stores
ithin the Tufton Centre,
longside the South Mall
ands Ashford House,
hree floors of self-
ontained office space.
enants have included
shford Chamber of
ommerce and
ccountants Finn Kelcey
nd Chapman.

Centre Square, the Tufton Centre, 1975. Here is another view of the Tufton Centre shortly after it opened.

Centre Square, the Tufton Centre, looking south-east from Lewis & Hyland's, 1975. Tesco Home 'n' Wear can be seen to the right and Foster's menswear, who previously had a shop in the High Street, is to the left of Tesco. Foster's former shop had been at 110 High Street, one of the properties demolished to make way for this development. Many will remember the three oast house-style kiosks, which sold tobacco and confectionery, jewellery and flowers.

Centre Square, the Tufton Centre, 1975. Looking towards the South Mall on a busy shopping day, Dolcis shoes can be seen on the left, Tesco and Foster's Menswear on the right. Just inside the South Mall are Adams childrenswear, Trueform Shoes, Harris Carpets and Ashford Audio. None of these tenants have premises here today.

South Mall, the Tufton Centre, 1975. Bell-bottom trousers were particularly popular at the time. Notice the gentleman nearest the camera in a suit: whatever happened to kipper ties?

OFFICES &
SHOWROOMS
TO LET
HEALEY & BAKER
Burrows
ASHFORD
THE TUFTON CENTRE
AERO
Milk Chocolate
Adorabubble
Autumn Collection
JOHN FARMER

Upper High Street, 1975. This view shows the High Street entrance to the Tufton Centre just after its completion. The front entrance was substantially altered in 1989 when the Tufton Centre was refurbished and renamed County Square.

Centre Square, the Tufton Centre, 1990. The centre remained open throughout 1989 and 1990, during the refurbishment works. Here the crane can be seen lifting steelworks for the new covered glass roof into place. Most of the heavy work was undertaken on a Sunday, to limit disruption.

South Mall, County Square, June 1990. The change of name came almost overnight and was put into effect even before the refurbishment was completed. This view shows the South Mall looking north towards the Centre Square. At one point the scaffolding and hoarding made it particularly dark for shoppers.

Centre Square, County Square, May 1990. This view was taken from the office window of Ashford Chamber of Commerce, located in Ashford House at the time. It shows the main steelworks that supported the huge covered glass roof.

High Street, 1991. The completed High Street entrance to the County Square shopping centre. As this book goes to press further plans are being looked at to extend the centre over the Godinton Road car park area.

High Street, 1969. This unusua building, built in 1967 for J. Sainsbury, replaced the chain' overcrowded store at 18 High Street, breaking their tradition c counter service in the town. Th glass-fronted design was a specification for most of their new self-service stores in the 1960s and came as a novelty to many customers. The International Stores further along the High Street extended its store at about the same time, to follow the trend. This store o the site of the former Saracen's Head Hotel, which was demolished in 1966, was deemed to be too small by the mid-1970s. In 1978 a new one opened behind in Park Street.

High Street, 1987. In 1979, a year after J. Sainsbury moved to Park Street, Boots the Chemist moved fro their smaller store further up the High Street (now W.H. Smith) into the former supermarket. The glas fronted design has disappeared in favour of Boots' more traditional look. (*R.G. Salter*).

ɟinburgh Road, 1977. This view from the Ringway ɿows the back of the third Sainsbury's store. It was ɔnstructed by Canterbury firm, Wiltshiers, on land wned by Charter Consolidated Ltd, an international ɔd local mining finance company. The new store, ɿown as Park House, opened in 1978, together ith a multi-storey car park.

ırk Street, 1978. The Park Street Sainsbury's store ı opening day. This store was enlarged in 1986 as ırt of the Park Mall shopping centre, but it closed 2001 although still successful. The staff moved to e Bybrook store in Simone Weil Avenue, which ɔened in August 1992, and their old shop became a 'ilkinson Superstore in 2002. Ashford Borough ɔuncil now runs the multi-storey car park.

Lower High Street, 1976. Headley Brothers' grocer business was established in 1848. Shortly after thi 1976 photograph was taken the business ceased trading, and 46 High Street was extensively redeveloped. Retaining the original fascia design, the shop was transforme into Headley Brothers' stationery and art supplies business, which included a sub-post office This business continued to trade until 1988, after 108 years in the High Street. No. 46 is now home to a McDonald's franchise.

Edinburgh Road, 9 March 1984. Although it is difficult to imagine today, this is the view from the roof Sainsbury's multi-storey car park, looking towards New Street. Following the opening of the Ringway November 1974, this land, which contained properties in the path of the Ringway, fell into decay. The stre passing through the centre of the photograph was Wolseley Road and further back towards New Street w Park Road. The derelict houses in the foreground were in Edinburgh Road. The owners of this land, Chart Consolidated, were urged to tidy up, which they did, and in 1986 work commenced on the Park Ma shopping centre.

Wolseley Road, 1984. An elevated view from the roof of Woolworth's, showing the derelict Park Street site at its junction with Wolseley Road. The two buildings illustrated on the site belonged to Geering's of Ashford.

Stone Street, 1984. Following the construction of Sainsbury's in Park Street, Stone Street, which ran parallel with the Ringway, was used as an access road for the multi-storey above Sainsbury's. The exit road from the car park was Edinburgh Road. This arrangement changed when the shopping centre was completed.

Park Street, 1977. Before Park Mall was built Park Street was still a through road, serving as the back entrance to premises in the Upper High Street. Here the rear access to Woolworth's and Geering's is seen on the right. The street had been widened earlier in 1973.

Park Road, 1977. Showing a scene not instantly recognisable today, this picture was taken outside the New China City Restaurant in Park Road, looking towards Castle Street. Folkestone Glass was one of the last remaining businesses on this site before the construction of the shopping centre.

Park Road, 1983. This view from twenty years ago shows the Kengate Beasley 3 Day Cleaners at 2 Park Road next to the New China City Restaurant. The lean-to building to the left of the cleaners was Baldwin's, the tool sharpeners and key cutters. At the very end of Park Road nearest the Ringway the Vacuum Centre had a busy showroom. None of the businesses is still operating today.

Park Street, 1986. The building of the new Park Mall shopping centre is well under way. This picture was taken from Sainsbury's multi-storey car park. Months later Park Street was severed by the new centre. Traffic had to be diverted, as this was previously a through road to the Ringway.

Edinburgh Road, 1986. Looking alongside Sainsbury's in Park Street, where Edinburgh Road had previously stood, we can see the foundations being put in place for the new shopping centre. As this site was once occupied by houses and businesses, it was not unusual to discover numerous underground air-raid shelters of reinforced concrete construction, which hampered the workmen.

Upper High Street, 1986. The former Curtess shoe shop at 88–90 High Street was incorporated into the Park Mall development. During its reconstruction a workman using a blowtorch accidentally set light to the original oak timbers, many of which were replaced by pine. On completion nos 88–90 became part of the entrance to Park Mall, and has been Cloud's, the greeting card and gift shop, since the centre opened in 1987.

Park Street, February 1986. Park Street is no longer a through road in this view, taken from the rear of the George Hotel. The extension to Sainsbury's is nearly complete, but the main centre has some way to go before completion.

Park Street, September 1986. Sainsbury's and its multi-storey are seen here shortly before the completion of the new shopping centre. During the building works Sainsbury's continued trading despite sections of the supermarket being closed off. This was done with minimal disruption.

Park Mall shopping centre, 1987: an early view of the partially completed centre, taken from outside the Sainsbury's extension. Traders have yet to occupy the new shop units.

Park Mall High Street entrance, September 1987. The shops occupying the attractive High Street entrance to the shopping centre in September 1987 are Barratt's shoes and The Jewellers Guild. Barratt's are still trading on the site today.

Upper High Street, 1977. International supermarket in the autumn of 1977 at 92–94 High Street. K Shoe shops are to the left and Curtess shoes to the right. International had been trading on the site for many years before extending their store in 1968.

Upper High Street, 1987. This was taken from the same position as the 1977 photograph, when Park Mall was still under construction. Incidentally, the young boy in the centre outside the entrance is the author aged thirteen.

Upper High Street, 1997. What a difference ten years can make! The attractive entrance to Park Mall shortly after its tenth anniversary in September 1997.

Aerial view, 12 April 1988. It is difficult to estimate the difference the development made until you're in the air. This view shows the Upper High Street at the bottom, Park Mall shopping centre in the middle and the Ringway running along the top of the picture.

3

Charter & its Contribution

Kent House, 1970. In 1967 international mining finance company Charter Consolidated came to Ashford. This was a British company with substantial investment holdings and subsidiaries in many countries, its head office situated in London. Mining interests covered most of the metals and minerals in use in those days including coal, copper, diamonds, gold, iron ore, lead, nickel, platinum, potash, silver, tin, uranium, wolfram and zinc. Today Charter is no longer as large as it was, but still has an office in London. These offices in Station Road were the company's first Ashford premises, which it eventually outgrew. Eurostar and the Employment Service are now the main occupants of the building. (*Lambert Weston*)

North Street, 15 December 1971. In 1969 Charter Consolidated purchased 3.7 acres of land owned by Metropolitan Estates to the rear of North Street, with a view to transforming it into its new Ashford office. At the time the controversial plans were met with much opposition. The final outcome was a nine-storey office block rising approximately 120 feet above ground level. This view illustrates the rear of properties in North Street. (*Lambert Weston*)

Charter site, 15 December 1971. Looking towards Somerset Road, this view shows the site before construction work began. A footpath within the site, which once ran diagonally from Somerset Road to Wellesley Road, was eventually totally obliterated by the giant office complex. (*Lambert Weston*)

North Street, 15 December 1971. This grand old town house, 22 North Street, which was once owned by two Misses Lepard, is shown from the rear before its extensive garden was swallowed up by the construction works. This and many other buildings in North Street were later extensively refurbished. No. 22 has now been converted into flats. (*Lambert Weston*)

Left: North Street, 1971. These ecclesiastical arches and windows were uncovered during the land clearance to the rear of 30 North Street. It is thought that they were erected by Dr Wilks, a one-time owner of the house. Owing to a misunderstanding when the land was being cleared, it is believed that they were removed and disposed of, along with waste rubble. The culprits were subsequently sent to retrieve them. *Right:* North Street, 1971. Here is the arched doorway discovered at the back of 30 North Street. (*Lambert Weston*)

The junction of Somerset Road and Wellesley Road, 15 December 1971. Resembling a bombsite, this view is taken looking towards Mace Lane, while the houses and gardens were cleared to start building Charter House. The Trumpeter Inn (now Domino's Pizza) is seen on the left, while the office building further down, on the corner of Wellesley Road and Mace Lane, is the tax office. The row of attractive houses in the centre was later demolished for the Ringway. (*Kentish Express*)

Somerset Road, 1971. This uninterrupted view of Somerset Road looks towards North Street after the demolition of properties for the Ringway. The brick wall lined with trees formed the footpath, which ran from Somerset Road to Wellesley Road. The houses were subsequently demolished for the forthcoming Ringway. The large house seen in the distance (centre) is 22 North Street. (*Lambert Weston*)

Charter site, 24 November 1972. The basement, ground- and first-floor sections of the north wing can be seen here during the early stages of construction. Somerset Road is on the right. (*Weavers/Countrywide*)

Charter site, 1972. The extensive foundations are apparent in this detailed view, looking towards North Street and the Lower High Street. St Mary's Church is in the background. (*Lambert Weston*)

Charter site looking towards Wellesley Road, 2 October 1972. The enormous foundations of Charter House are starting to take shape here. The building's helicopter rotor-shape can be seen clearly, as can (beyond the rails for the crane on the right of the picture) the car park at the back of the County Hotel, which in those days was much bigger than today. (*Lambert Weston*)

The junction of Wellesley Road and Somerset Road, 2 October 1972. This excellent pre-Ringway view, taken from the roof of the Crown Building (the tax office), shows the full extent and size of the site from a prime position. It was less than a year earlier that the site had originally been cleared. Massive McAlpine cranes dominate the site and rather dwarf St Mary's Church, which can be seen to the left. The Ringway now skirts the foreground. (*Lambert Weston*)

Charter site, 9 January 1973. It is hard to believe today this was the main entrance to Charter House in its early stages of construction. More importantly, Park Street now passes along the right of the picture. (*Weavers/Countrywide*)

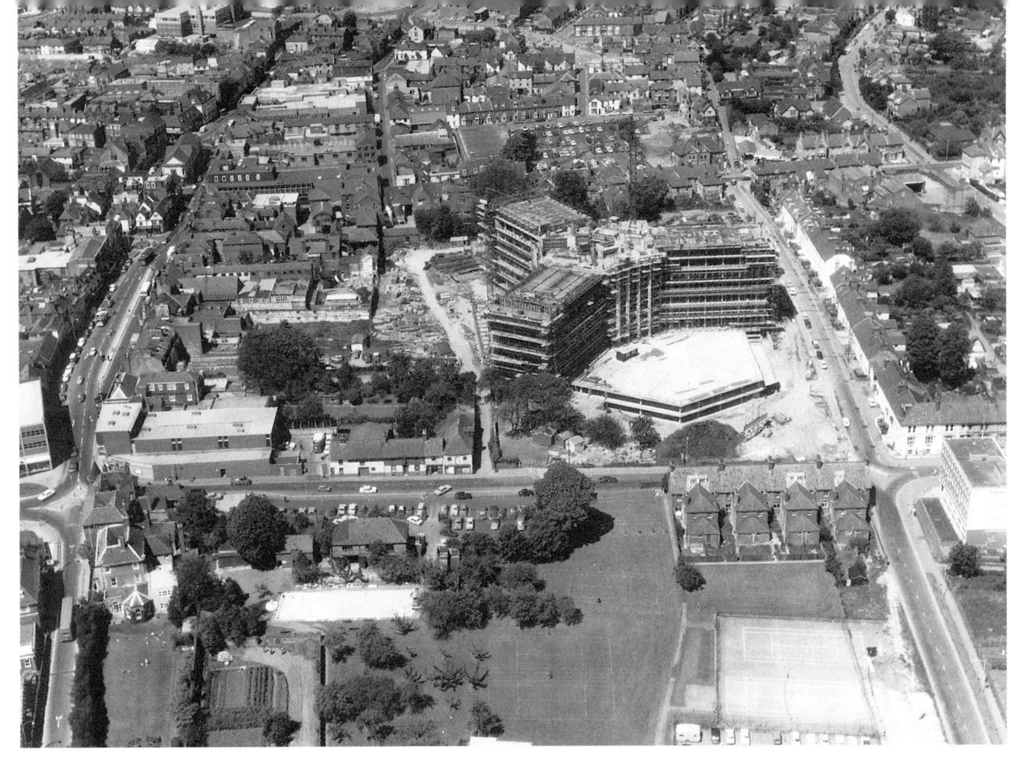

Aerial view, looking east and showing Charter House two years before its completion, 1973. At the top of the picture the construction of the Ringway is under way. The junction of Somerset Road, Wellesley Road and Mace Lane can be seen on the right, and the junction of the High Street, East Hill and Station Road on the left. Notice the direction of the traffic in those days. (*FotoFlite*)

Aerial view, looking west towards Willesborough, 1973. This view again shows Charter House (top), while Somerset Road and Mace Lane are to its left. North Street, Edinburgh Road, Wolseley Road, Stone Street and Park Street can be seen in the bottom left-hand corner of the picture and the High Street and Kings Parade dominate the right. East Hill Mill is at the top of the picture. (*FotoFlite*)

Aerial view, looking north, 1973. Charter House (centre) dwarfs the Lower High Street at the bottom of the picture. Before the Ringway was built North Street was a through road, joining the A28 Canterbury Road towards Kennington. The Ashford bypass (completed in 1957) is shown running from left to right at the extreme top of the picture. (*FotoFlite*)

Charter House, 16 October 1973. The topping out ceremony took place on a cold, wet day in October 1973. Those present were the chairman of Charter Consolidated Ltd, Sidney Spiro, and the managing director of Sir Robert McAlpine & Partners, Ken Gibson. Here Sidney Spiro and his wife arrive from the hoist to carry out the ceremony. (*Lambert Weston*)

Charter House, 16 October 1973. McAlpine contractors line up the cement bucket, while Ken Gibson of McAlpines walks across to Sidney Spiro with a spade and float to polish off the wet cement. Among the group of senior officials from Charter and McAlpine are Mr M.B. Hofmeyr, managing director of Charter, and Arthur Ley of Ley Colbeck & Partners, architects. (*Lambert Weston*)

Charter House, with the surrounding Ringway nearing completion, 1974. The Somerset Arms public house, on the corner of Somerset Road and North Street, has disappeared, as has the Lord Roberts public house in North Street and Emetco in Wellesley Road. The latter was demolished for the Park Street service road. (*Weavers/Countrywide*)

SPD
INTERNATIONAL

Charter House, 18 May 1975. Charter House, Park Street and most of the Ringway have been completed, but Wellesley Road is still not finished at its junction with the Lower High Street. (*Weavers/Countrywide*)

Charter House, 26 February 1975. This view, taken from the roof of the tax office in Wellesley Road, show Charter House shortly before its final hand-over to Charter Consolidated. This section of the Ringwa although not complete, has partially opened to traffic. (*Lambert Weston*)

Charter House, 1975. This is the south side of the building a few months after the first occupation by sta who had moved from Kent House and Charter's other temporary offices in the town. (*Lambert Weston*)

'ark Street, 1975. From a photographer's point of view Charter House, taken from close proximity, can reveal n unusual effect. This view shows the imposing but futuristic structure at its best. (*Weavers/Countrywide*)

harter House, 1975. Sidney piro, Chairman of Charter onsolidated Ltd, arrives for the fficial opening. The buildings in ie background are those in the ower High Street. (*Weavers/Countrywide*)

Charter House, 1975. Sidney Spiro toasts the opening, with the mayor, Cllr Peter G. Boulden, and other senior company colleagues and local representatives. (*Weavers/Countrywide*)

Charter House, 1975. During the opening ceremony Sidney Spiro shows colleagues and local people the model of Charter House and its future proposed development interests. (*Lambert Weston*)

Charter House, 1975. One of the tastefully designed reception areas in Charter House, shortly after its opening. (*Lambert Weston*)

Kent House, 1974. Shortly before moving to the new Charter House conditions in Kent House were cramped. Trailing telephone cables are an accident waiting to happen. Interestingly this is the year the Health and Safety at Work Act came into operation. (*Weavers/Countrywide*)

The in-house print room at Kent House, 1974. (*Weavers/Countrywide*)

Charter House, 1975. Young women are using the microfiche readers in the spacious new offices. (*Weavers/Countrywide*)

Charter House, 1975. Charter's stylish 1970s office suite contained 242,000 square feet of office space. Once Charter had moved back to London, ten years after opening its Ashford premises, this luxurious complex was never fully used again. (*A'Court Photographs Ltd*)

Somerset Road, 1980. Old and new: the effect of Charter House on the residents of Somerset Road can be seen clearly here.

Park Street, 6 July 1973. Once a quaint thoroughfare, Park Street was later widened in line with Charter's creation of a new service road, which involved the demolition of properties and businesses along the right of this photograph. The George Hotel is on the left, together with its garage on the right. Further along on the right, R. Dean, the turf accountant, can be seen at the junction with Edinburgh Road. The row of houses next door was once known as Postman's Row. (*Lambert Weston*)

Park Street, *c.* 1973. Further along Park Street on the right stood Tom Camier's Motor Cycles and Henlys, the Wolseley dealer. These businesses were also demolished as part of the plans to widen roads in the area. The Old Prince of Wales public house can be seen in the distance. (*Roy Entwistle*)

Park Street, 6 July 1973, photographed from the rear of Woolworth's and International, looking towards New Street. In Wolseley Road on the right (outside Henlys) a 1972 Hillman Hunter is for sale, priced at £1,195 – expensive for a year-old car in 1973. The Park Mall shopping centre now covers this whole area. (*Lambert Weston*)

North Street, 1973. This dramatic photograph was taken from the roof of Sainsbury's (now Boots) before the severance of North Street at its junction with Somerset Road. The Lord Roberts public house, previously the Red Lion, can be seen next door to Denne, the seed merchants. On the opposite side of the road John Hogbin, the estate agent, sits on the corner of North Street and Park Street. Both Hogbin's and the Lord Roberts were demolished shortly after this picture was taken, as part of the road-widening scheme. (*Lambert Weston*)

Park Street, December 1974. The road-widening scheme has started in earnest. Tom Camier's, Henlys and Postman's Row have already disappeared, changing the face of Park Street for good. In the distance the new road surface is being laid while vehicles negotiate their way past. The houses on the right are already empty, ready for the bulldozers to move in.

Park Street, December 1974. This view was taken from Park Road, looking towards Charter House. Part of the Folkestone Glassworks showroom has had to be demolished to accommodate the new road. New Street is behind the camera and Castle Street is on the right.

The junction of Park Street and North Street, 1975. The new service road passes through where the old Lord Roberts public house once stood. W.H. Gibbs, the house furnishers and removal contractors, are seen on the left, while the flank wall on the right is that of Denne, the seed merchants. The two-storey building behind W.H. Gibbs has since been demolished. (*Lambert Weston*)

Park Street, 1975. The new service road can be seen looking towards New Street. The North Street car park is on the right; it has now been turned into an office complex. (*Lambert Weston*)

North Street before pedestrianisation, looking towards Middle Row and St Mary's Church, 1975. W.H. Gibbs is on the immediate left, while Denne, Hobbs Parker, estate agents, and Ashley Russell Ltd can be seen further along on the left. At the junction of North Street and the High Street, the Mocha Bar and Milbet's the butcher can be seen either side of the passageway to the church. The building on the right, formerly the site of the Saracen's Head Hotel, is Sainsbury's and Roger Britton Carpets, now Boots and Save the Children respectively. (*Lambert Weston*)

Park Street, 19 December 1977. This was Park Street nine years before the Park Mall shopping centre divided it up. The fenced-off area on the left later became Ashford's third Sainsbury's supermarket, which opened in 1978.

Park Street, 1977. Looking towards New Street, this view shows the rear of Woolworth's and International after the street-widening scheme had come into effect. International was demolished in 1986 to create the entrance to the Park Mall shopping centre. The area of road in the foreground is now a turning place for delivery lorries and taxis.

North Street, 1972. These fine old properties in North Street were those purchased by Charter Consolidated Ltd when they acquired the land from Metropolitan Estates in 1969 to construct Charter House. Nos 16–18, 20, 22, 24 and 26 North Street, together with the properties on the opposite side of North Street, were found on purchase to be in a bad and dilapidated state, and most had been uninhabited for some time. Charter therefore took on the task of refurbishing these properties to give them a new lease of life. (*Weavers/Countrywide*)

North Street, 6 April 1972. On the opposite side of North Street work is under way on the offices of Harrison Clague, architects, and Dresden, hairdressers. The car park to the right of the building was redeveloped in the late 1980s and the offices of the *Kentish Express* now stand there. (*Weavers/Countrywide*)

North Street, 17 January 1972. Next to 22 and 24 North Street were two small shops, nos 26 and 28. The front of no. 26 (now Hydra House) was declared unsafe by the Urban District Council, and had to be demolished and rebuilt in keeping with the architectural style of the upper part of the building. The shops were once C.E. Parish, the grocers, and R. & I. Dancey's, the 'invisible' tailors. (*Weavers/Countrywide*)

North Street, 26 November 1973. No. 30 can be seen here prior to its conservation and redevelopment. The Army Careers Centre occupied the left-hand side of these premises, and the shop on the right was Cross's, the graphic art supplier. The shop is today occupied by Formative Fun. (*Lambert Weston*)

North Street, 26 June 1973. The fronts of 16 and 18 North Street are pictured here before their redevelopment. Next door is the Olde Cottage Restaurant, which has changed hands over the years and is now known as the Little Raj. Ashford Sports later occupied nos 16 and 18, and for a number of years has been the Coliseum photographic studio and gift shop. (*Lambert Weston*)

North Street, 1973. This was once a rather deceptive property externally. No. 9 North Street had previously been Fendall's, the wine merchant, and when it came to refurbishing the property it was found that the second-floor windows were false. They were later put to use in the construction of a dormer. The property is currently the Anatolian Restaurant. (*Lambert Weston*)

North Street, 1975. The Olde Cottage Restaurant at 20 North Street is one of the oldest buildings in Ashford. The late Walter Briscall, who was a recognised authority on the history of the town, created the original painting above the door. He was most annoyed when it was altered somewhat unprofessionally to accommodate the change of name. (*Lambert Weston*)

North Street, 18 July 1973. Here is the kitchen attached to the Olde Cottage Restaurant, clearly in desperate need of modernisation. It was later transformed, making it much easier to keep clean. (*Lambert Weston*)

North Street, 18 July 1973. Another view of the kitchen at the Olde Cottage Restaurant. (*Lambert Weston*)

North Street, 1973. These Tudor cottages, situated behind 16–18 North Street, were in a terrible state when purchased and had a demolition order hanging over them. They had been uninhabited for a number of years, so the task that faced Charter was tremendous. This picture shows the cottages in the early stages of redevelopment. (*Lambert Weston*)

North Street/Knotts Square, 1973. This is the quaint courtyard to the rear of 16–18 North Street, known as Knotts Square, before the redevelopment works. (*Lambert Weston*)

Nos 20, 22, 24, 26, 28, 30 and 32 North Street, 6 April 1972. In early 1972 no. 26 was in a sorry state, but just under three months later the frontage has been totally rebuilt. The row of terraced properties adjacent to the lamp-post was later demolished for the Ringway. (*Weavers/Countrywide*)

North Street, 15 May 1974. This view shows the interior of 20 North Street after refurbishment and alterations to the bar. (*Lambert Weston*)

North Street, 15 May 1974. Here is another view showing the interior of 20 North Street after refurbishment and alterations to the dining-room. (*Lambert Weston*)

The refurbished frontage of 16–18 North Street, 1975. The walkway to the side of the building is the access to Knotts Cottages. (*Lambert Weston*)

North Street/Knotts Square, 14 October 1974. Knotts Cottages had been superbly transformed, together with the lovely communal garden. Upon refurbishment the cottage on the right created an extension to no. 20, the Olde Cottage Restaurant. (*Lambert Weston*)

Knotts Square, 1975. Charter's chairman Sidney Spiro, his wife and Mr M.B. Hofmeyr, Charter's managing director, take a tour around Knotts Square as part of their inspection of the refurbished properties in North Street. (*Lambert Weston*)

North Street, 5 June 1973. Taken from the bus stop in North Street, this photograph shows the refurbishe frontages of 26 and 28 North Street. No. 26 is now known as Hydra House and no. 28 is now the Nort Street doctor's surgery. (*Lambert Weston*)

4

The Infamous Ringway is Born

The junction of North Street and Somerset Road, 22 June 1973. Before the advent of the Ringway Ashford was a series of one-way streets, like Somerset Road. Several properties and public houses were sacrificed to make way for the Ringway, which, like Charter House, caused much controversy among locals. This view taken in North Street at its junction with Somerset Road shows the Somerset Arms public house on the left and the Tunbridge Wells Equitable Friendly Society on the right. The Ringway now sweeps from the left into Somerset Road, from Kennington. The houses on the left further down are still standing today. (*Lambert Weston*)

North Street, 22 June 1973. Across the road, this photograph is taken through the forecourt of Chambers Garage, which was for many years owned by Mr Leo Chambers. Today the garage is much bigger and is now situated on the corner of the Ringway and North Street. The Somerset Arms public house can be seen on the left at the junction with Somerset Road, which is now the site of Ashdown Court. Charter House is in the centre, under construction. (*Lambert Weston*)

West Street, 1974. Only a small section of West Street still survives today. The telephone exchange can be seen at the top of the street where it joins Forge Lane. The former Salvation Army hall on the right was demolished in about 1993, and the site has remained derelict ever since. (*Lambert Weston*)

North Street, 21 March 1973. This picture, taken from the junction of Somerset Road and North Street, shows nos 32–33, shortly before demolition. This is where the Ringway passes through. (*Lambert Weston*)

Somerset Road, 22 June 1973. A pre-Ringway look at Somerset Road, taken from the top of the crane during the construction of Charter House. McAlpine's offices can be seen on the left. Blue Line Lane is opposite the junction of Somerset Road, running alongside Chambers Garage. (*Lambert Weston*)

Edinburgh Road before the Ringway cut through, 1972. Hollington private school is on the right, and the rear of Geering's stationers and printers can be seen in the distance. The road now terminates just past the house on the left with the black and white timber gable end, and has been renamed Hollington Place. Hollington School has since closed.

Godinton Road, 1974. The road was still two-way when this picture was taken. The houses on the right have already been demolished for the Ringway and the Salvation Army hall can be seen behind the rubble. Upon the opening of the Ringway East Street on the right was made a no through road. The Amoco garage on the left, later Elf, closed in 2002. (*Kentish Express*)

Forge Lane, 1972. The drainage pipework for the Ringway surrounds C.J. Anderson's (also known as Mancini), scrap metal merchants in Forge Lane, which has already closed pending demolition. Work has started on the Ringway, which eventually realigned Forge Lane further towards New Rents. (*Kentish Express*)

Station Road, 1972. Here is another forgotten group of properties, now the site of the Royal Mail sorting office. Many of the houses and businesses are boarded up, awaiting demolition. Some of the businesses that once traded from this spot were reputable Ashford traders, such as A.J. Sharp, electrician, Henry S. Roberts (Kingston) Ltd, Thanet School of Motoring, and a tobacconist. The Ashford Working Men's Club can be seen further along on the left next door to Crouch's Garage, on the corner of Dover Place. Ashford station is far right, next to the Kent Arms public house on the left. (*Roy Entwistle*)

Godinton Road, 1972. The office complex on the corner of Gasworks Lane and Godinton Road is under construction here, next to the Amoco filling station. Club Q snooker club and the Ashford Fabric Warehouse now occupy the complex.

Station Road, 1973. Taken from the junction of East Hill, this picture shows a much narrower Station Road with Greencoat and Kanthack House on the left. The old East Kent Road Car Company garage, which was demolished in 1997, can be seen further along on the left. The *Kentish Express* newspaper once occupied Greencoat House, before moving across the road to Pearl Assurance House. East Hill was closed to through traffic upon the opening of the Ringway. Hoskins, the tobacconist, used to stand immediately left.

Looking north-east along the inner Ringway from its junction with Kent Avenue, 6 July 1973. The houses in Park Road are being demolished, creating something of a bombsite in the process. This was a typical scene in Ashford between 1972 and 1974. (*Lambert Weston*)

Forge Lane, early 1972. An interesting pre-Ringway view of Forge Lane. The British Flag public house on the right was demolished shortly after this photograph was taken. The telephone exchange can be seen in the centre. (*Kentish Express*)

Forge Lane, late 1972. This shows the kerbstones being laid for the realigned Forge Lane section of the Ringway. F.G. Bradley, the yeast merchant and bakers' sundriesman, can be seen on the left, at the top of New Rents.

North Street, 1974. Cars negotiate their way through the roadworks in North Street at its junction with Hardinge and Albert Roads, during the construction of the Ringway in 1974. The building on the left was later demolished for the Ashdown Court development. On the far right is the Masonic Temple: this is where the road was later terminated for the construction of the Ringway. (*Kentish Express*)

Opposite above: Stone Street, 1973. The remains of Wolseley Road after demolition had taken place to make way for the Ringway are seen both to the left and right in this view taken from the top of Stone Street. Chambers Garage can be seen to the left of the houses in Somerset Road (centre) and the old *Ashford Advertiser* office is seen below the crane at Charter House on the right. Park Mall shopping centre now covers the area to the right of the Ringway. (*Roy Entwistle*)

Opposite below: The junction of Somerset Road and North Street, 25 January 1974. Here is the new Ringway during the early stages of construction. The Somerset Arms has gone, together with the Tunbridge Wells Equitable Friendly Society on the opposite corner of Somerset Road. Houses have been demolished in North Street, Edinburgh Road, Wolseley Road, Park Road and Kent Avenue. (*Lambert Weston*)

WALLIS

Ringway construction, 20 February 1974. The rubble from the old houses has been cleared away to reveal the new road surface before it was opened to traffic. The flank walls to the houses have been replaced where the houses adjacent had once stood. Park Road, between the temporary fences, is still a through road, but not for much longer. Charter House is seen nearing completion, behind the *Ashford Advertiser* office on the right. (*Lambert Weston*)

Ringway construction, 22 October 1973. A superb shot of North Street at its junction with Somerset Road, prior to the complete demolition of those properties in the path of the Ringway. Chambers Garage can be seen on the left, while, opposite, the roof slates on the Somerset Arms have been removed and the name has been painted out. The Masonic Temple (right) is in North Street next door to the Army Careers Information Centre. The Tunbridge Wells Equitable Friendly Society (centre) later moved to Wolseley Road after their premises were demolished. (*Lambert Weston*)

Kent Avenue, 1973. This is another view of the Ringway under construction, at the corner of Kent and Sussex Avenues. The houses on the right were originally in Park Road, Wolseley Road and Edinburgh Road. They were demolished in the late 1970s. (*Lambert Weston*)

New Street, 1973. New Street was widened as part of the Ringway construction. Norwood Gardens and Barrow Hill can be seen in the centre, and Caffyn's Garage on the right.

Forge Lane, 1973. Taken from the Gravel Walk car park, this illustration shows the finished section of the Ringway in Forge Lane. The building on the right is the telephone exchange. A crane from the Tufton Shopping Centre development can be seen to the left.

The Ringway, 19 November 1974. This is the finished Ringway looking east towards Somerset Road. Since opening, the Ringway has acquired the image of a 'Brands Hatch'-type racetrack. The author was ten days old when this picture was taken. (*Lambert Weston*)

Edinburgh Road, December 1974. The houses on the right remained until 1985, when after standing unoccupied for several years they were demolished to make way for Park Mall shopping centre, while the car park on the left made way for Sainsbury's new store in 1977.

Park Road, December 1974. Here is a severed Park Road where it joined the Ringway in the early 1970s. The remains of the street no longer exist, and again made way for the Park Mall development.

Wolseley Road, December 1974. Wolseley Road once passed through this section of the Ringway. It has since been renamed Wolseley Place, and was once the home of local photographers Richard and Ken Carley and their business, Wolseley Place Studios.

Ringway, 1977. The road is seen here at its junction with North Street, three years after completion. Charter House dominates the picture, while the properties in North Street can be seen on the right.

The Ringway, 1977. Sainsbury's new supermarket in Park Street can be seen under construction by local Canterbury firm Wiltshiers. Charter House is on the left, together with North Street.

The junction of Church Road and Elwick Road when Elwick Road was still accessible from the Ringway, 1977. This was renowned for being an accident blackspot, and was later made a no through road. Ashford market is just up on the left.

The Ringway, 1982, before the construction of Park Mall shopping centre.

ACKNOWLEDGEMENTS

Over the years many local people and companies have been extremely kind and patient in assisting me with my research. In particular, many have given valuable information, which has enabled me to collate an interesting record of the history of Ashford and build a substantial photographic collection. I would therefore like to give special thanks to the following individuals and companies:

Richard Filmer of Halifax Property Services, Arthur Coleman, Mike Bennett, Dave Downey and Barry Hollis at the Kent Messenger Group, Kent Regional Newspapers (Ashford office), Arwen Turner, David 'Taffy' James, Harry Chainey and Peter Thwaite at Charter, Betty Shadwell, Brenda and George Sharp, Tom Hall, Richard Carley, photographer, Clague Architects, the late Walter Briscall, Linda Robards and Shirley Sheridan at Ashford Library, Adrian Westwood at Ashford Borough Council, Phil Neumann at FotoFlite, Ian Gambrill of Countrywide Photographic, Charing, the late Colin Harding of Campbell, Reith and Hill, the late Dennis Shadwell, celebrated photographer with the Kent Messenger Group, Richard Stafford at Colyer Commercial, Chris West at Ashford Town Partnership, Alan Fuller Photography of Medway, Cllr Gordon Turner, Clive Langley of GA Group, Don Entwistle at CIN Properties, Roy and Maureen Entwistle, Donald Samuel, Will Kenny and Rob Prince at Luminar Leisure (Liquid and Life, Ashford) and Nick Brown of South Ashford.

Thanks are also due to anyone whose name has not been acknowledged either through an oversight or because the original source or present ownership is unknown or unavailable. Also, not forgetting a big thanks to Simon Fletcher at Sutton Publishing for making this happen, and making a childhood dream come true.